Animal Kingdom

CRUSTACEANS

by Emma Carlson Berne

Consultant: Jackie Gai, DVM
Wildlife Veterinarian

raintree

a Capstone company — publishers for children

Raintree is an imprint of Capstone Global Library Limited, a company incorporated in England and Wales having its registered office at 264 Banbury Road, Oxford, OX2 7DY – Registered company number: 6695582

www.raintree.co.uk
myorders@raintree.co.uk

Edited by Kathryn Clay
Designed by Rick Korab and Juliette Peters
Picture research by Kelly Garvin
Production by Gene Bentdahl
Originated by Capstone Global Library LTD
Printed and bound in China.

ISBN 978 1 4747 3456 1
21 20 19 18 17
10 9 8 7 6 5 4 3 2 1

British Library Cataloguing in Publication Data
A full catalogue record for this book is available from the British Library.

Acknowledgements
We would like to thank the following for permission to reproduce photographs:Alamy: Design Pics, 31 (bottom right), Jeff Rotman, 30 (right); Minden Pictures: Flip Nicklin, 27 (top), Fred Bavendam, 16 (middle), 24 (top left), Richard Herrmann, 27 (bottom); Newscom/Andrey Nekrasov/NHPA/Photoshot, 19 (bottom left); Shutterstock: Adrian Kaye, 24 (top middle), Aleksey Stemmer, cover, (br), Andrea Izzotti, 26 (t), 31 (tl), Andrey_Kuzmin, 4-5, Antonio S, 30 (left), antos777, 1, (l), aodaodaodaod, 6 (t), ARTRAN, 24-25, bcampbell65, 20-21, Ben Queenborough, 18 (br), Bildagentur Zoonar GmbH, 23 (b), bluehand, 29 (t), BMJ, 19 (br), D. Kucharski K. Kucharska, 28 (l), devil79sd, 29 (b), Dmytro Pylypenko, 7 (t), 26-27, Ethan Daniels, cover (bl), 14 (t), eye-blink, 18-19, FCG, cover (top right), fish1715, 13 (t), Gena Melendez, 1 (r), Geza Farkas, 5 (b), Greg Courville, 10-11, Gonzalo Jara, 12-13, Henrik Larsson, 15 (m), IanRedding, 14 (b), 28-29, Ivan Kuzmin, 31 (bl), javarman, cover (tl), Jennifer White Maxwell, 18 (tr), JGA, 20 (t), Joseph Calev, 31 (tr), Kiwisoul, 19 (tl), ksi, 25 (tm), LagunaticPhoto, 22-23, Lebendkulturen.de, 17 (m), Lia Caldas, 6 (b), littlesam, 16-17, llyashenko Oleksiy, 18 (tl), Martin Fowler, 23 (t), mastersky, 18 (bl), Mati Nitibhon, 25 (bm), Mauro Rodrigues, 28 (r), Mr.TJ, 13 (b), Nathan Litijens, 24 (b), nicefishes, 5 (t), Nicholas Piccillo, 7 (b), Nora Yusef, 32, onsuda, 27 (m), Palo_ok, 7 (bm), Passenier, 12 (t), PNSJ88, 25 (b), Puripat, 7 (tm), RossHelen, cover, 1, (bkg), Rostislav Ageev, 17 (b), S_E, 8-9, Seaphotoart, 14-15, Stubblefield Photography, 24 (tr), Tatyana Domnicheva, 4 (b), think4photop, 15 (b), Trieu Tuan, 24 (bm), Under The Sea, 6-7, Vagabonddivan, 19 (tr), Videologia, 17 (t), wanchai, 12 (b), Warakorn Buaphuean, 25 (t), Ye Choh Wah, 15 (t)

Artistic elements: ducu59us, Markovka, Mascha Tace, mr.Timmi

Artistic Elements: Shutterstock: Fotonium, Krivosheev Vitaly, Panu Ruangjan, Zubada

CONTENTS

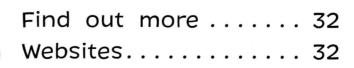

What are crustaceans?

Crustaceans are animals that live mostly in water. They have shells and many legs. Lobsters, crabs and shrimp are well-known crustaceans.

class
a smaller group of living things; crustaceans are in the class Crustacea

phylum
(FIE-lum)
a group of living things with a similar body plan; crustaceans belong to the phylum Arthropoda (ar-THROP-uh-duh); insects and arachnids are also in this group

kingdom
one of five very large groups into which all living things are placed; the two main kingdoms are plants and animals; crustaceans belong to the animal kingdom

order
a group of living things that is smaller than a class; there are at least five orders of crustaceans

cold-blooded
also called ectothermic (EK-tuh-THER-mik) cold-blooded animals have a body temperature that is the same as the air around them; crustaceans are cold-blooded

invertebrate
(in-VUR-tuh-brut) an animal without a backbone; crustaceans are invertebrates

arthropod
(AR-thruh-pod) an invertebrate with many body sections; crustaceans, insects and spiders are arthropods

species
(SPEE-sees) a group of animals that are alike and can produce young with each other; there are more than 50,000 species of crustaceans

Getting into groups

Crustaceans come in all sizes, from the giant king crab to tiny krill. Some are even too small to see with the human eye!

crab
a type of shellfish with a hard shell, four pairs of legs and two large front claws called pincers; crabs can live in water or on land

shrimp
a crustacean with many pairs of legs and a fan-shaped tail; most shrimp live in the ocean

lobster
a large shellfish that lives in the ocean; lobsters have a hard shell, pincers and eyes that stick out from their head

barnacle
(BAR-nuh-kuhl): a crustacean with a rock-like outer shell; barnacles glue themselves to rocks, ships or other animals

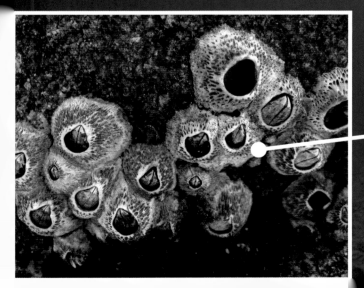

krill

an animal that looks like a small shrimp, with a shell and many pairs of legs; krill are an important food source for whales, large fish and birds

crayfish

also called a crawfish or crawdad; crayfish look like small lobsters and live in freshwater

decapod

a type of crustacean with 10 legs; crabs, shrimp, crayfish and lobsters are decapods

isopod

a type of small crustacean with seven pairs of legs; woodlice are isopods

Take a look

Most crustaceans have bodies made up of three parts: head, thorax and abdomen. Hard shells protect crustaceans' bodies.

exoskeleton
(EK-so-SKEL-ih-ton) the hard covering that protects the inner parts of animals without backbones; all crustaceans have exoskeletons

thorax
(THOR-aks): the middle part of the body; on some crustaceans, the head and thorax are stuck together and covered with a large shell

abdomen
(AB-duh-muhn): the end part of the body; the tail is part of the abdomen

carapace
(KAR-uh-peys): the hard shell that covers the head and the thorax

head
the part of the body that holds the brain and sensing organs

compound eye
many tiny eyes that work together to see; crustaceans and insects have compound eyes

mouthpart
a small limb or structure around the mouth; mouthparts are used to grab food and suck it in

gill
a body part used to breathe under water

All about appendages

Snapping jaws. Pinching claws. Some crustacean body parts might look scary. But they are important for swimming, grabbing and sensing.

swimmeret
a leg used mainly for swimming; some animals use their swimmerets to help them move or hold eggs

mandible
(MAN-duh-buhl): a jaw-like organ used to bite prey and chew food; crustaceans have two mandibles

antenna
(an-TEN-uh): a long, thin body part used to smell and feel; crustaceans have two sets of antennae

maxillae
(mak-SIL-ee): helper jaws that pass food to the mandibles and aid in grooming; crustaceans have one or two sets of maxillae

appendage
(uh-PEN-dij): a part of an animal that sticks out from the main body; legs, claws, jaws and antennae are appendages

claw
a hard body part used for gripping or holding things; crabs and lobsters use their claws to fight and to break apart shells

From young to adult

Crustaceans lay eggs. Some lay their eggs in water. Others carry the eggs until they hatch.

life cycle
the series of changes that take place in a living thing, from birth to death

egg
most crustaceans lay eggs in the water; crayfish carry eggs on their swimmerets until their young hatch

mate
to join together to make young; banded coral shrimp mate with only one partner their whole lives

lifespan
the number of years a certain animal usually lives; many crustaceans can live up to 30 years; some lobsters and crabs can live as long as 70 years

larva
(LAR-vuh)
a crustacean that has hatched from its egg

moult
to shed; when crustaceans get too big for their exoskeleton, they crawl out; the old one is replaced by a larger one

A place to call home

Most crustaceans live in the ocean. But some, like crayfish, live in freshwater streams and rivers. A few crustaceans even live on land.

habitat
the type of place and conditions in which a plant or animal lives

aquatic
(a-KWA-tik): relating to animals that live in water; most crustaceans are aquatic

forest
an area with many trees; woodlice live in cool, shady forests and under rocks

salt water
water that is salty; salt water is found in oceans

ocean

a large body of salt water; most crustaceans live in the oceans and along the shores

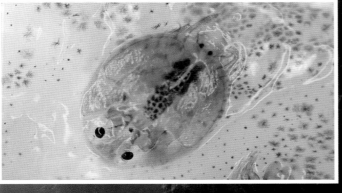

freshwater

water that does not contain salt; most ponds, rivers, lakes and streams are freshwater bodies

parasite

an animal or plant that lives on or inside another animal or plant; tongue worms and fish lice are parasites

farm

a place where plants and animals are raised for eating; some shrimp are raised on farms

Dinner time

Many crustaceans eat other animals. But some munch on plants or bacteria.

omnivore
(OM-nuh-vor): an animal that eats both meat and plants; crayfish eat fish and small plants called algae

prey
(PRAY): an animal hunted by another animal for food; sea urchins, starfish and clams are prey for large lobsters

predator
(PRED-uh-tur): an animal that hunts other animals for food; most crustaceans are predators

scavenger
(SKAV-in-jer): an animal that feeds on animals that are already dead; hermit crabs will eat almost anything they find

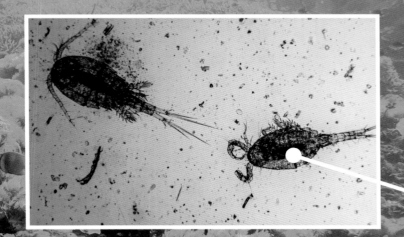

water flea

plankton
tiny plants and animals that drift in the water; shrimp and krill eat plankton

bacteria
(bak-TEER-ee-uh): tiny, one-celled organisms that live on plants and animals; water fleas eat bacteria

nocturnal
(nok-TUR-nuhl): active at night; most crustaceans spend the day buried in the sand, under rocks or in underwater caves; they search for food at night

A bit crabby

About 4,500 species of crab exist. Some are as small as a bean. Some are larger than an adult human.

blue crab
a type of crab with bright blue claws; blue crabs are about 10 to 23 centimetres (14 to 9 inches) long

stone crab
a grey, medium-sized crab with powerful claws that lives in the Gulf of Mexico

pea crab
a tiny crab about the size of a pea; they live as parasites inside clams and mussels

cast
a group of crabs

pincers

the first pair of a crab's legs or claws

hermit crab

a type of crab that lives either on land or in the sea; hermit crabs do not have a shell of their own; they live inside empty shells left by sea snails

king crab

a large crab with long, spiny legs that lives mainly in cold seas; king crabs can look like spiders as they walk on the ocean floor

bristle

a hair around a crab's mouthparts that helps with smelling and tasting

Learning about lobsters

Lobsters are some of the largest crustaceans. They continue to grow for their entire lives.

clawed lobsters

one of two main groups of lobsters; they have two big pincers at the front of their bodies; there are about 30 types of clawed lobsters; American lobsters are the most common

regenerate

(ree-JEN-uh-rate): to grow again; lobsters can regenerate their legs, antennae and claws if they lose one

gastric mill

an organ right behind a lobster's eyes; also where a lobster's stomach is located; the gastric mill contains bones and teeth that grind food

burrow

a tunnel or hole in the ground made or used by an animal; lobsters dig burrows on the ocean floor

colour

lobsters are red only after they are cooked; live lobsters can be yellow, orange, white, grey, blue or brown; chemicals in a lobster's shell react to cooking heat, turning the shell red

sensor
a body part that responds to temperature, light, sound or motion; lobsters have sensors on their antennae that help them find prey in the dark

telson
the central tail fan; lobsters can quickly escape predators by moving backwards with a flip of their telson

spiny lobsters
the other main group of lobsters; spiny lobsters live in warm oceans and do not have big claws

Stuck like a barnacle

Barnacles are unlike most crustaceans. They don't have claws or legs. They stick to rocks and gather food through an opening in their shell.

glue
barnacles make a type of sticky glue to attach themselves to surfaces in the ocean

filter
to pull in a liquid to get something out of the liquid; barnacles filter water to feed on the tiny bits of food floating in it

cirri
(SIR-ee)
the narrow, wispy arms or appendages of a barnacle; barnacles reach out and scoop food from the water with their cirri

whelk
a type of sea snail that eats barnacles

cluster
a group of the same things all together; barnacles often grow in clusters all over rocks, ships and other hard surfaces under the water

sessile
(SES-il)
staying in one place; barnacles are sessile once they grow their shell plates

plate
a hard, flat shell; plates protect barnacles from predators

Show me shrimp!

Shrimp are curved creatures with legs to spare. Five legs help them to walk. Five others help them swim.

prawn

a type of crustacean that looks like a large shrimp; prawns can measure 15 to 20 cm (6 to 8 inches) long

banded coral shrimp

also called cleaner shrimp; they help fish by eating away parasites and dead tissue

mantis shrimp

a strong shrimp that uses its powerful claws to crush the shells of prey; mantis shrimp claws can break glass and cut through bone

whiteleg shrimp

a type of shrimp found mainly in the Pacific Ocean; this is the kind most people eat

fairy shrimp

tiny, see-through shrimp that live in freshwater ponds

flex

to bend; shrimp flex their bodies to quickly move backwards when predators are nearby

wild shrimp

shrimp that live in the oceans; they're caught with nets or boat machinery

trawling

a kind of fishing in which a large net is dragged across the bottom of the ocean; wild shrimp are caught by trawling

farmed shrimp

shrimp raised in water farms or pens

brine shrimp

tiny shrimp that live in salty lakes and seas; flamingoes get their pink colour from eating brine shrimp

King krill

Krill look like tiny shrimp. They're small in size, but they play a big role in the ocean's food chain.

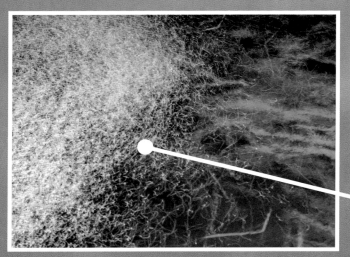

swarm
a group of krill

biomass
(BI-oh-mass): the amount of living things in one area; krill are the most plentiful animal species on the planet

keystone species
an animal on which other animals depend for food; whales, seals, squid and some birds eat krill or eat other animals that eat krill

algae
(AL-jee): small plants without roots or stems; ice algae grows in snow and ice; krill eat it

global warming
the warming up of Earth's land and oceans; as the oceans warm, there is less ice algae for krill to eat

phytoplankton
(FIE-toe-plank-ton) single-celled ocean creatures; krill eat phytoplankton that drift near the surface of the ocean

food chain
a series of living things in which each one eats the one before it; krill are a food source for many animals

Think small

Lobsters and crabs are easy to spot. But these tiny crustaceans might be missed.

ectoparasite
(EK-toe-PAR-uh-site)
a type of parasite that lives outside of the body of the animal it feeds on; sea lice are ectoparasites

sea louse
a small crustacean that feeds off the blood and skin of fish and whales

woodlouse
also called a pill bug or roly-poly bug; woodlice live on land under rocks or in other damp places and sometimes roll up into a ball when threatened

copepod
(KOH-puh-pod)
a type of tiny crustacean no larger than the point of a pencil

pleopod
(PLEE-uh-pod)
the leg on a
crustacean that is used
mainly for swimming;
woodlice use their pleopods
for walking and breathing;
their legs have breathing
organs in them

seahorse
a fish with a
horse-shaped head
that feeds on tiny
crustaceans

**head
louse**
an insect that is
not related to sea
lice or woodlice

**water
flea**
a tiny crustacean
that lives mainly in
small freshwater pools;
when water fleas
swim, they look like
hopping fleas

Fun facts

The **largest lobster** ever caught was 20 kilograms (44 pounds). It was about 1.1 metres (3.5 feet) long.

Lobsters have clear blood. But it turns blue when exposed to air.

Lobsters sometimes carry their eggs on their bodies for up to one year.

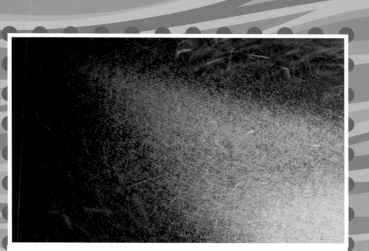

Astronauts can see masses of **krill** from space.

Some species of **krill** have bodies that glow in the dark.

Woodlice have many nicknames, including pill bugs and roly-poly bugs. They are also called armadillo bugs, sow bugs, lockchests, cheesybobs, coffin-cutters and pea-bugs.

Some **crabs** are right-clawed, and some are left-clawed. Male fiddler crabs use either their right or left claws for fighting other males.

Some **king crabs** have a leg span that is 1.8 m (6 feet) across.

FIND OUT MORE

British Seashore (Nature Detective), Victoria Munson (Wayland, 2015)

Crafty Crustaceans (Creatures of the Deep), Heidi Moore (Raintree, 2011)

Seashore (Fact Cat Habitats), Izzi Howell (Wayland, 2015)

WEBSITES

animals.nationalgeographic.com/animals/invertebrates/lobster
Facts about lobsters with photographs.

easyscienceforkids.com/all-about-crustaceans
Visit this website for more information about crustaceans.

www.sciencekids.co.nz/sciencefacts/animals/crab.html
This website has fun facts about crabs.